TABLE OF CON™

...TED

...S

C, B, A SONGS

5 FINGER ORIGINALS

5 FINGER CLASSICS

CHORD OUTLINE

PARALLEL MOTION

CHORD PATTERN

RHYTHM

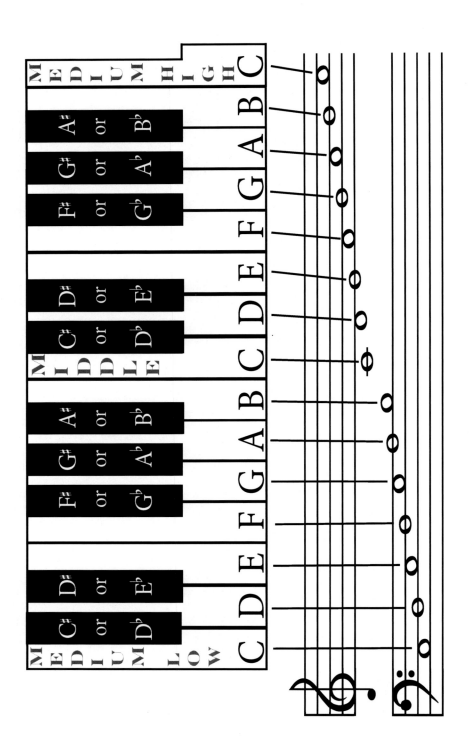

Treblemakers Piano Method
GETTING STARTED

- Here's the first lesson. This should help you and your teacher cover everything you need to know to begin reading and playing right away.

- You may want to cut out flash cards (found in "Treblemakers Piano Tools") before you begin.

- There's a lot of information in this lesson, but you'll be using it over and over until you know it well.

- By the end of this lesson you will be playing your first song by reading the notes yourself!

- Following the tips throughout the book will:
    1. Help you avoid common mistakes and build good habits.
    2. Let you know when to add flash cards and rhythm cards.
       (found in "Treblemakers Piano Tools")
       ### LET'S GET STARTED!

1. MUSICAL ALPHABET:

- **The letters A through G of the alphabet are used to name the different notes in music.**

- **Play A through G on the piano, naming the notes as you go.**

- **Don't forget... in music, the alphabet starts over again after G.**

2. SETS OF BLACK KEYS:

- **There are sets of 2 and 3 black keys on the piano.**
  (and also one single black key at the bottom end of the piano)

- **Show where all of the sets of 2 black keys are on the piano.**

- **Show where all of the sets of 3 black keys are on the piano.**

- **Can you see how the black and white keys make a pattern that repeats?**
  (That means that notes of the same name will look the same on the piano, just higher or lower.)

3. MIDDLE C, D, E ON THE PIANO:

Middle C on the piano

- The first note that we are going to learn on the piano is called Middle C.

- It is in the middle of the piano right below the set of two black keys.
  (Hint: It is usually under the label of a piano or keyboard)

- Remember that the other C keys will look the same.

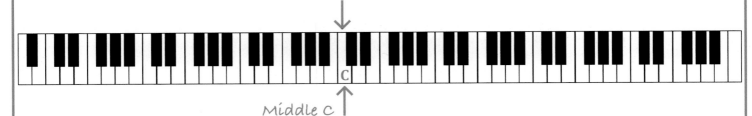

Middle C

- Can you find the other C keys on the piano? Look below the other sets of two black keys.

- The highest C is the only one that doesn't have two black keys above it since it is the last key on the piano. Play this C.

D on the piano

- D is between the the two black keys.

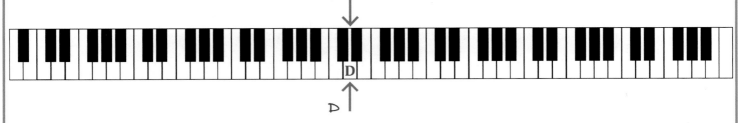

D

- Can you find the other D keys on the piano?

E on the piano

- E is above the two black keys.

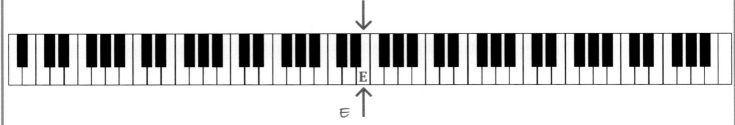

E

- Can you find the other E keys on the piano?

4. THE STAFF:

- This is a staff. Symbols, like notes or clefs, are put on the staff to show what to play.

- Add the staff flash card to your pile of flash cards to practice.

5. TREBLE CLEF:

- This is a treble clef. Treble means high.

- When a treble clef is placed on the staff, it tells you to play the higher part of the piano. (usually from Middle C on up)

- Show the higher part of the piano.

- Add the treble clef flash card to your pile of flash cards to practice.

6. BASS CLEF:

- This is a bass clef. Bass means low.

- When you see a bass clef on the staff, it tells you to play the lower part of the piano. (usually from Middle C on down)

- Show the lower part of the piano.

- Add the bass clef flash card to your pile of flash cards to practice.

7. LINES & SPACES STAND FOR NOTES:

- **Every line and space on the staff stands for a note on the piano.**
- **Starting with Middle C, draw a note on every line and space of the staff.**

- **Label each note.**

 **SPACE NOTES:** Notes that sit in the spaces of the staff between two lines.

- **These are space notes.**   - **Draw notes on all of the spaces of the staff.**

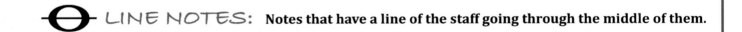

 **LINE NOTES:** Notes that have a line of the staff going through the middle of them.

- **These are line notes.**   - **Draw notes on all of the lines of the staff.**

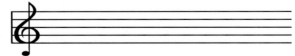

QUIZ

- **Say whether the following notes are line notes or space notes.**

8. MUSIC IS A PICTURE:

- **Music is a picture of what is played on the piano.**

UP ↑

- **When the notes go up on the page, they go up on the piano.**

- **Point to the notes as they go up the page.**
- **Play notes going up the piano.**

DOWN ↓

- **When the notes go down on the page, they go down on the piano.**

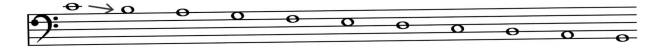

- **Point to the notes as they go down the page.**
- **Play notes going down the piano.**

 DRAWING NOTES

THIS CAN BE A GREAT WAY TO SOLIDIFY UNDERSTANDING OF WHERE THE NOTES ARE ON THE STAFF.

 SPACE NOTE:
1. **Put point of pencil on the line at the top of the space.**
2. **Circle around setting it on the line below.**

 LINE NOTE:
1. **Put point of pencil in the middle of the space above the line.**
2. **Circle around through the middle of the space below.**

(Line goes through middle of note like a marshmallow on a stick.)

Teacher/Parent Pointers:

- *Draw the Middle C ledger line for student.*

- *Have student draw the note. Make sure they are seeing the difference between lines and spaces.*

- *Young students often draw huge notes that go over several lines and spaces.*
  Guide them to keep drawing notes "a little smaller" until they get to the right size.

- *Try letting them trace one of your notes first.*

- *Make a dot where the pencil point should go to START drawing the note.*

9. MIDDLE C, D & E ON THE STAFF:

MIDDLE C

• This line is Middle C.

• It doesn't matter what the note looks like, if it's on this line, it's Middle C.

(What kind of note you put on the line will tell you how long to hold the note, but don't worry about that yet.)

whole note   half notes   quarter notes   eighth notes

• Take out matching flash card.   **• Set card on music stand and play Middle C.**

• Draw a line of Middle C notes. Middle C is one ledger line below the staff in treble clef.

D

• This space is D.

whole note   half notes   quarter notes   eighth notes

• Take out matching flash card.   **• Set on music stand next to C and play D.**

• Draw a line of D notes.

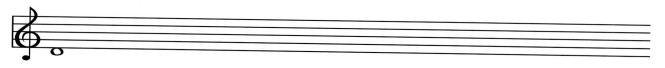

E

• This line is E.

whole note   half notes   quarter notes   eighth notes

• Take out matching flash card.   **• Set on music stand next to D and play E.**

• Draw a line of E notes.

10. QUIZ ON PLAYING & READING C, D, E WITH RIGHT HAND:

- **Find the set of two black keys in the middle of the piano under the label.**

Label

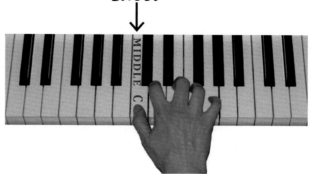

- **Put right hand one finger per key starting with thumb on Middle C.**
- **Sitting position: Always center body in front of Middle C .**
- **Place flash cards on music stand in C, D, E, order.**

- **Play the note and say the note name out loud as your teacher points to the card.**

  (Use finger that already resting note. Don't switch to a different finger.)

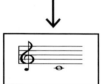  

Teacher/Parent Instructions on Quizzing: (Make sure student uses correct fingers.)
1. *Go forward a few times: C, D, E.*
2. *Go backwards a few times: E, D, C.*
3. *Go forwards and backwards.*
4. *Quiz on notes using only stepping. Example: C, D, C, D, E, D, C, D etc. until easy*
5. *Quiz on notes in any order.*
6. *Add C,D,E to flash cards to practice during the week. Leave the other cards in the 'Don't Add Yet' pile.*

PLAYING LEGATO: HOW TO CONNECT NOTES

- **Imagine your fingers are legs walking on the keys.**
- **Both legs can not be off the ground at the same time.** →

1. Put hand in position. 2. Press down first note. 3. Press down second note. 4. Let up first key.

READ YOUR FIRST SONG BY COMPARING NOTES:

1. IS IT A SPACE OR A LINE NOTE?

SPACE NOTE

D

LINE NOTE?

C or E

floating free like a planet

bottom line of the staff

WATCH ME READ

Watch me read
1   2   3   4

C,   D,   E
1   2   3   4

I   just   learned   these
1   2   3   4

notes   to - day
1   2   3   4

Can't   be - lieve
1   2   3   4

I   can   play
1   2   3   4

This   song   right   a -
1   2   3   4

way
1   2   3   4

After you can read the song with correct notes and fingers, add legato (pg 7) and rhythm (pg 61).

♩ quarter note = 1 count   ♩ half note = 2 counts   o whole note = 4 counts

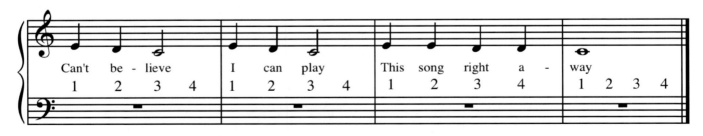

3 IMPORTANT HABITS!
1. **KEEP FINGERS IN ONE-FINGER-PER-KEY POSITION:** Use finger already on key! Don't switch!
2. **CONNECT YOUR NOTES:** Don't lift between notes!
3. **DON'T WRITE NOTE NAMES IN ON YOUR SONGS OR GUESS:** This prevents note-reading practice.

HOW TO PRACTICE:

- Play first phrase (I'm a furry little worm) 3x.
- If it doesn't sound smooth and feel easy, try 3 more.
- Once first phrase is smooth, move on to phrase 2 (All I do is eat).
- When phrases 1 and 2 are smooth, put them together.

BUTTERFLY

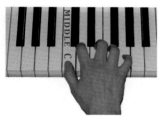

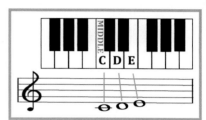

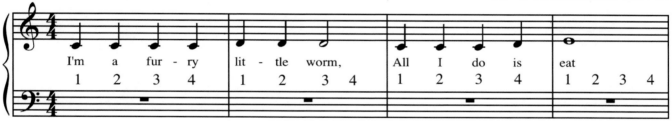

I'm a fur-ry lit-tle worm, All I do is eat
1 2 3 4   1 2 3 4   1 2 3 4   1 2 3 4

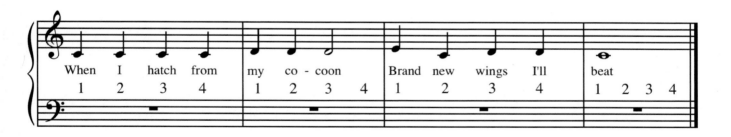

When I hatch from my co-coon Brand new wings I'll beat
1 2 3 4   1 2 3 4   1 2 3 4   1 2 3 4

DON'T FORGET! 3 IMPORTANT HABITS! DON'T FORGET!
1. KEEP FINGERS IN ONE-FINGER-PER-KEY POSITION.
2. CONNECT NOTES.
3. DON'T WRITE IN NOTE NAMES.

Teacher/Parent Pointers:
- *Give student a specific number of times to play a phrase. (3 or 5 usually)*
- *A specific number keeps it goal-oriented and helps teach students that repetition is part of learning.*

S'MORES

The line goes through the Mid-dle C like roast-ing marsh-mal - lows, yum-my!
1 2 3 4   1 2 3 4   1 2 3 4   1 2 3 4   1 2 3 4

Marsh - mal - lows go in - side s'mores while C's go in - side mus - ic scores
1 2 3 4   1 2 3 4   1 2 3 4   1 2 3 4

DON'T FORGET! **3 IMPORTANT HABITS!** DON'T FORGET!
1. KEEP FINGERS IN ONE-FINGER-PER-KEY POSITION.
2. CONNECT NOTES.
3. DON'T WRITE IN NOTE NAMES.

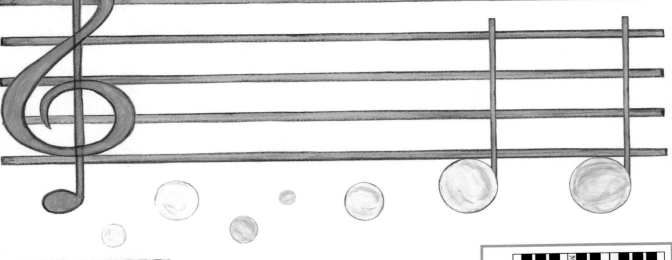

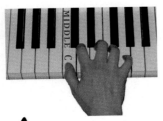

BUBBLES

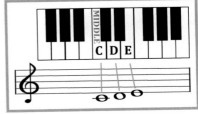

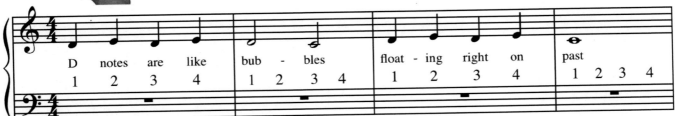

D notes are like bub - bles float - ing right on past
1 2 3 4 1 2 3 4 1 2 3 4 1 2 3 4

Then they have some trou - ble and stick to the staff
1 2 3 4 1 2 3 4 1 2 3 4 1 2 3 4

DON'T FORGET! **3 IMPORTANT HABITS!** DON'T FORGET!
1. KEEP FINGERS IN ONE-FINGER-PER-KEY POSITION.
2. CONNECT NOTES.
3. DON'T WRITE IN NOTE NAMES.

Artwork © 2016 Suzan Stroud

♩ quarter note = 1 count
♩ half note = 2 counts
○ whole note = 4 counts

BARK! BARK! BARK!

BARK, BARK, BARK!

Bark bark bark
1 2 3 4

bow wow wow
1 2 3 4

Bark bark woof woof
1 2 3 4

bow wow wow
1 2 3 4

Bark shush bark shush
1 2 3 4

woof woof hush
1 2 3 4

Dog - gie please be
1 2 3 4

qui - et now
1 2 3 4

IT'S TIME TO ADD RHYTHM!

- Go to the Rhythm section (back of the book) to learn about rhythm.
- Add rhythms to your old songs. (Don't forget to add ○ , ♩ , ♩ to flash cards.
- Go through and box the held notes in your songs like so:

DON'T FORGET! **3 IMPORTANT HABITS!** DON'T FORGET!
1. KEEP FINGERS IN ONE-FINGER-PER-KEY POSITION.
2. CONNECT NOTES.
3. DON'T WRITE IN NOTE NAMES.

Teacher/Parent Pointers: • *Add rhythm cards. (instructions & cards in "Treblemakers Piano Tools")*

Artwork © 2016 Suzan Stroud   Music © 2010 Suzan Stroud

PURR

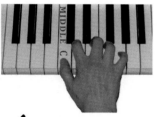

CATS ARE

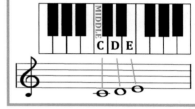

Cats — are / not so nois - y / They just / purr
1 2 3 4 / 1 2 3 4 / 1 2 3 4 / 1 2 3 4

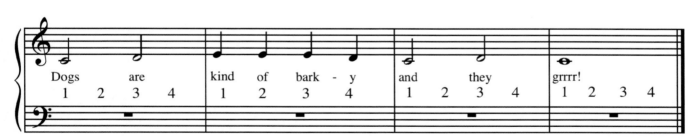

Dogs — are / kind of bark - y / and they / grrrr!
1 2 3 4 / 1 2 3 4 / 1 2 3 4 / 1 2 3 4

Don't forget! **3 Important Habits!** Don't forget!
1. Keep fingers in one-finger-per-key position.
2. Connect notes.
3. Don't write in note names.

Artwork © 2016 Suzan Stroud

Music © 2010 Suzan Stroud

13

STEPPING, SKIPPING & STAYING THE SAME

STEPPING: SKIPPING: STAYING THE SAME:

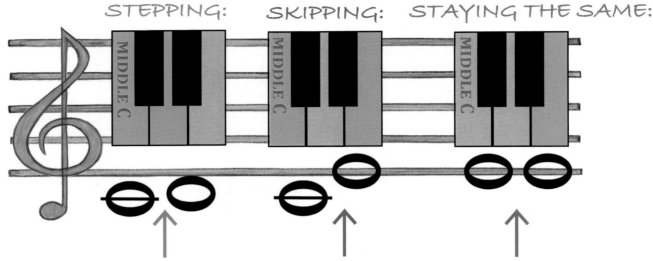

- One note to the next.
- Line to space or space to line on staff.
- Key to key on piano.
- Up or down.

- Line to line or space to space on staff.
- Skip over a key on piano.

- Notes stay the same.
- Same line or space of staff.
- Same key on piano.

STEP RIGHT UP

Step right up | Step right down | Hop and skip a | key

Look for step - ping | Look for skip - ping | It can help you | read

NAME STEP, SKIP OR STAYS THE SAME FOR EACH EXAMPLE BELOW?

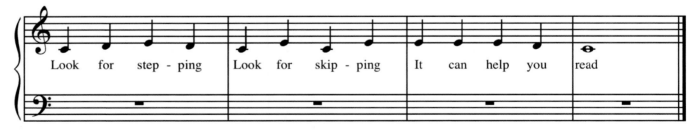

DON'T FORGET! **3 IMPORTANT HABITS!** DON'T FORGET!
1. KEEP FINGERS IN ONE-FINGER-PER-KEY POSITION.
2. CONNECT NOTES.
3. DON'T WRITE IN NOTE NAMES.

IMAGINE THE KEYS AS A PAIR OF STAIRS:

STEPPING:

- Imagine stepping from one step to the next.

SKIPPING:

- Imagine skipping a step.

STAYING THE SAME

- Imagine staying on the same step.

C, D, E SONGS

STEPPING, SKIPPING OR THE SAME

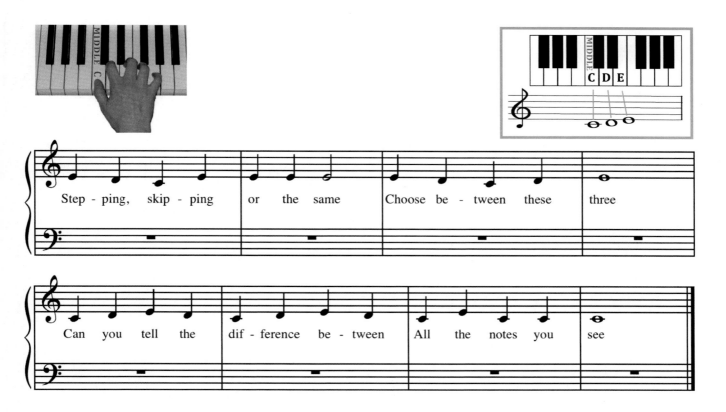

Step - ping,   skip - ping | or   the   same | Choose be - tween   these | three

Can   you   tell   the | dif - ference be - tween | All   the   notes   you | see

Don't forget! **3 Important Habits!** Don't forget!
1. Keep fingers in one-finger-per-key position.
2. Connect notes.
3. Don't write in note names.

RIDING

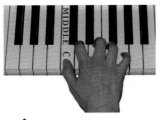

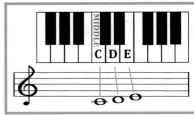

Rid – ing   glid – ing   on the side - walk   smooth

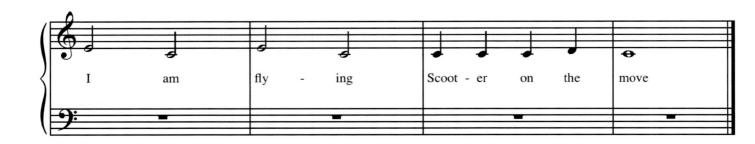

I   am   fly – ing   Scoot - er   on   the   move

DON'T FORGET! **3 IMPORTANT HABITS!** DON'T FORGET!
1. KEEP FINGERS IN ONE-FINGER-PER-KEY POSITION.
2. CONNECT NOTES.
3. DON'T WRITE IN NOTE NAMES.

WEAR YOUR HELMET

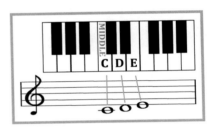

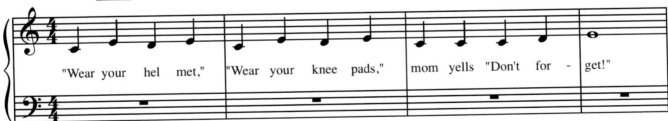

"Wear your hel met," "Wear your knee pads," mom yells "Don't for - get!"

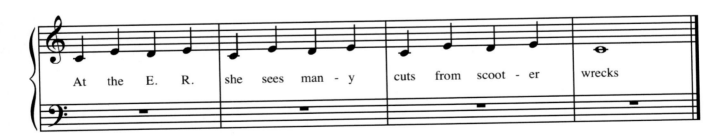

At the E. R. she sees man - y cuts from scoot - er wrecks

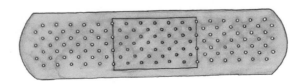

1. C, B, A ON THE PIANO & STAFF:

- **This is C, B & A with Left Hand on the piano.**
- **When you go down on the piano you have to go backwards in the alphabet!(C,B,A)**

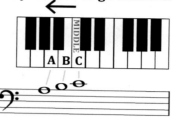

2. MIDDLE C POSITION LEFT HAND:

- **Put Left Hand in Middle C position.**

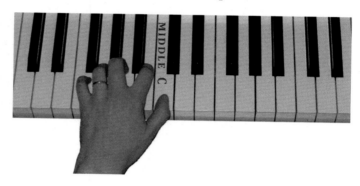

3. QUIZ ON READING & PLAYING C, B, A LEFT HAND:

- **Take out flashcards A, B & C.**
- **Place flash cards on music stand in A, B, C order.**

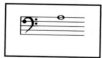 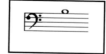 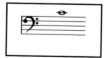

- **Put your fingers in the correct position.** (see picture above)
- **Play the note and say the note name out loud as your teacher points to the card.**
  (Use the finger that is already resting on the note. Don't switch to a different finger.)

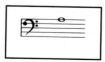 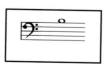

Teacher/Parent Instructions on Quizzing: *(Make sure student uses correct fingers.)*
  1. *Go backwards a few times: C, B, A.*
  2. *Go forwards a few times: A, B, C.*
  3. *Go forwards and backwards.*
  3. *Quiz on notes using only using stepping. Example: C, B, C, B, A, B, C, B etc. until easy.*
  4. *Point to notes in any order.*

DOWN WE GO

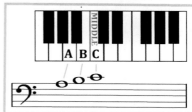

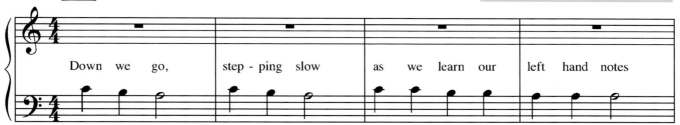

Down we go, | step - ping slow | as we learn our | left hand notes

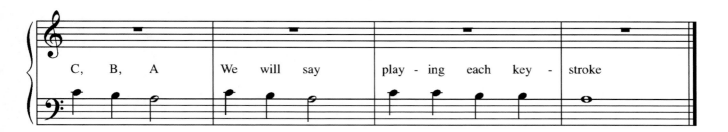

C, B, A | We will say | play - ing each key - | stroke

DON'T FORGET! **3 IMPORTANT HABITS!** DON'T FORGET!
1. KEEP FINGERS IN ONE-FINGER-PER-KEY POSITION.
2. CONNECT NOTES.
3. DON'T WRITE IN NOTE NAMES.

BIG BAD WOLF

C, B, A SONGS

DOTTED HALF NOTE ♩. = 3 counts

(Don't forget to add dotted half note ♩. to your flash cards.)

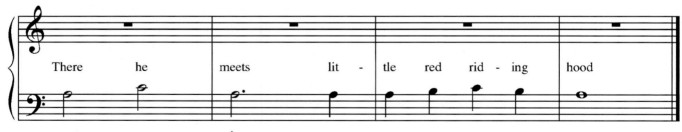

DON'T FORGET! **3 IMPORTANT HABITS!** DON'T FORGET!
1. KEEP FINGERS IN ONE-FINGER-PER-KEY POSITION.
2. CONNECT NOTES.
3. DON'T WRITE IN NOTE NAMES.

Artwork © 2016 Suzan Stroud   Music © 2010 Suzan Stroud

C, B, A SONGS

GRANDMA WHAT
BIG EYES

"Grand-ma what big eyes you have." "Grand-ma what big ears."

"Grand-ma what big teeth you have." "The bet-ter with to eat you my dear."

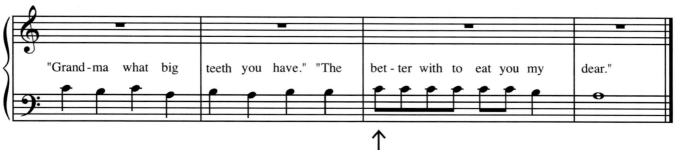

♪ **EIGHTH NOTES** ♫

- **Worth 1/2 a count.**
- **Single eighth notes:** ♪
- **Multiple eighth notes:** ♫ (stems turn into beams)
- **Twice as fast as quarter notes!**
- **Add eighth note rhythms to your Rhythm Cards.**

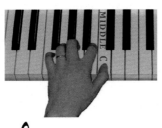

HUFF, HUFF, PUFF!

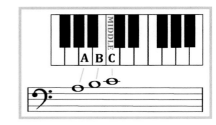

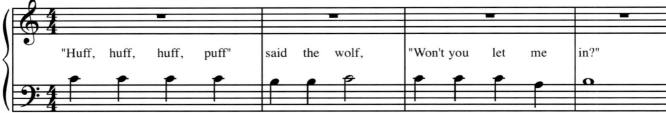

"Huff, huff, huff, puff" said the wolf, "Won't you let me in?"

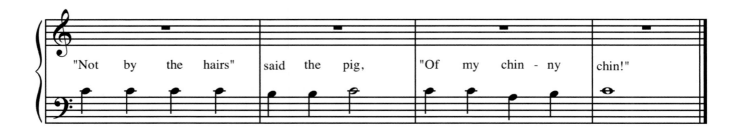

"Not by the hairs" said the pig, "Of my chin - ny chin!"

DON'T FORGET! 3 IMPORTANT HABITS! DON'T FORGET!
1. KEEP FINGERS IN ONE-FINGER-PER-KEY POSITION.
2. CONNECT NOTES.
3. DON'T WRITE IN NOTE NAMES.

C, B, A SONGS

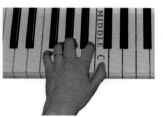

THREE LITTLE PIGS

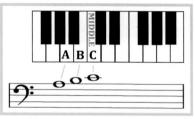

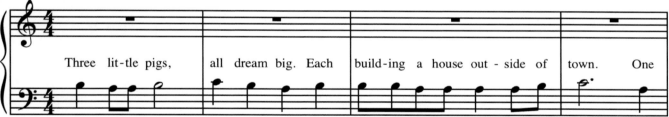

Three lit-tle pigs, all dream big. Each build-ing a house out - side of town. One

Dotted Half Note 𝅗𝅥. = 3 counts ↑

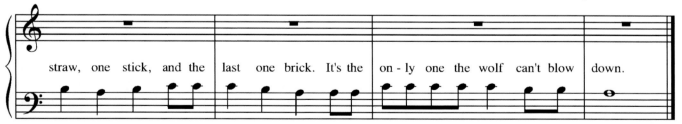

straw, one stick, and the last one brick. It's the on - ly one the wolf can't blow down.

• **Don't forget, eighth notes are twice as fast as quarter notes!**

C, B, A SONGS

TRA LA LA

Tra la la la | three goats frol - ick | look - ing for sweet | grass A -

cross the stream they | see grass green if | on - ly they could | pass

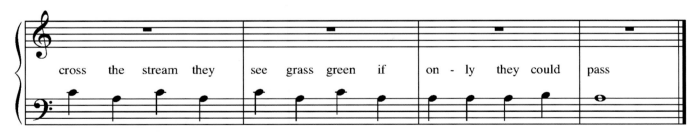

DOTTED HALF NOTE 𝅗𝅥. = 3 counts

Artwork © 2016 Suzan Stroud   Music © 2010 Suzan Stroud

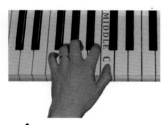

BELOW THE BRIDGE

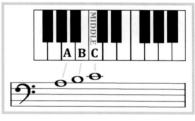

Be - low the bridge an | old troll lives | wait - ing for his | lunch

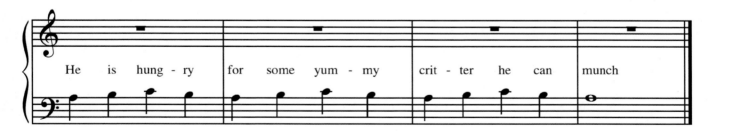

He is hung - ry | for some yum - my | crit - ter he can | munch

DON'T FORGET! **3 IMPORTANT HABITS!** DON'T FORGET!
1. KEEP FINGERS IN ONE-FINGER-PER-KEY POSITION.
2. CONNECT NOTES.
3. DON'T WRITE IN NOTE NAMES.

TRIP TRAP

1. Trip trap trip trap the troll says "Who's that tramp-ing on my bridge?" "Please don't eat me up." said the bil - ly goat gruff. "Here's my broth - er, he's twice as big."

2. Trip trap trip trap the troll says "Who's that tramp-ing on my bridge?" "Please don't eat me up." said the mid - dle goat gruff "Here's my broth - er, he's twice as big."

3. Trip trap trip trap the troll says "Who's that tramp-ing on my bridge?" Then the troll ran up and the big - gest goat gruff rammed the troll right in - to the riv - er.

DOTTED HALF NOTE ♩. = 3 counts

- These are repeat bars. Go back to the dots that face inward and play section again.
- Song repeats three times until all verses have been played.
- Follow verse lyrics after each number in order.

MIDDLE C POSITION: A-E

- COMBINE C, D, E IN RIGHT HAND WITH C, B, A IN LEFT HAND.
- PUT BOTH HANDS ON THE PIANO WITH THUMBS SHARING MIDDLE C. →

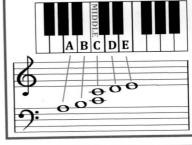

HIDE AND SEEK

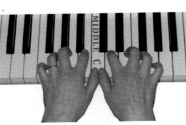

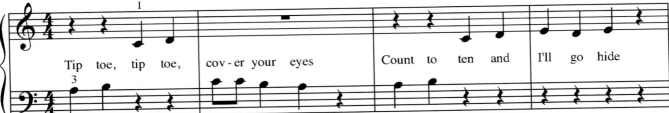

Tip toe, tip toe, | cov-er your eyes | Count to ten and | I'll go hide

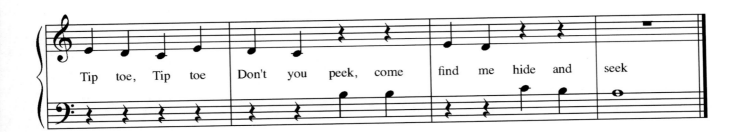

Tip toe, Tip toe | Don't you peek, come | find me hide and | seek

- **Leave both hands in position as you play so all of your fingers are ready when you need them.**
- **Don't forget to look at both staffs as the melody weaves back and forth like a snake!**

Artwork © 2016 Suzan Stroud

Music © 2010 Suzan Stroud

JUMPING ROPE

You two each can | take a side | Twirl the rope and | start the rhyme

Count-ing stead-y | I'll get read-y | Feel the rhy-thm then | I'll jump in.

- Notice when one hand has a rest, the other hand plays a note!
- Don't forget to add quarter rest 𝄽 to your flash cards.

RESTS
▬	Whole Rest	=	Rest for 4 counts
▬	Half Rest	=	Rest for 2 counts
𝄽	Quarter Rest	=	Rest for 1 count
♩/	Eighth Rest	=	Rest for 1/2 of a count

Artwork © 2016 Suzan Stroud

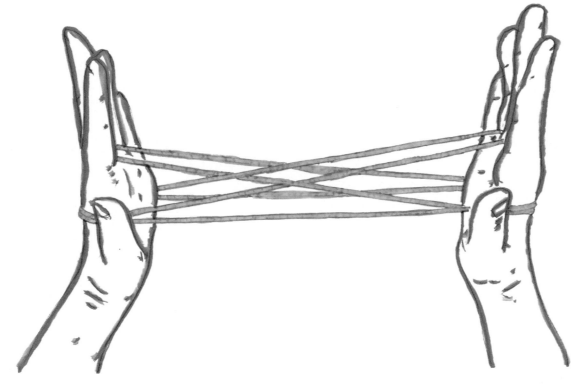

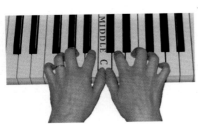

CAT'S CRADLE

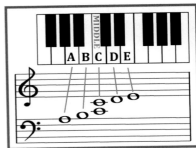

I string cats crad-le on my hands It's your move next since I be-gan

Pinch the X - es, ov - er, un-der "What shape is that?" We won - der

MARBLES

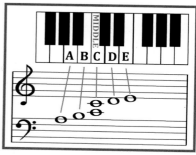

Make a cir - cle | with some string | Put the mar - bles | in the ring

Get your shoot - ers | read - y now | Shoot some mar - bles | out - side Pow!

30   Artwork © 2016 Suzan Stroud

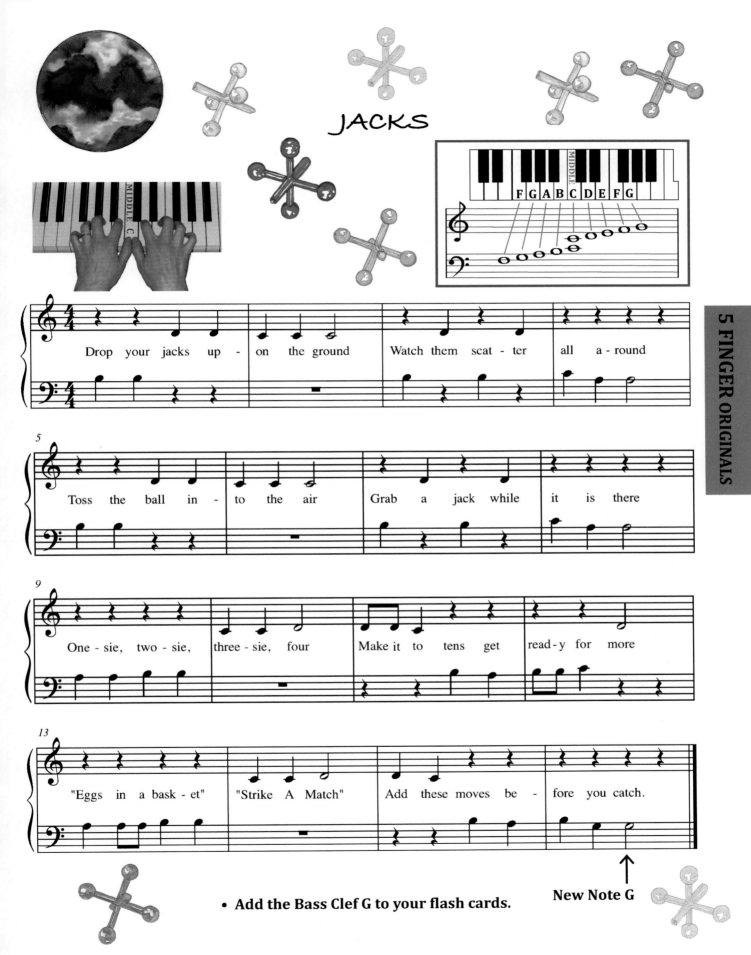

JACKS

HOP SCOTCH

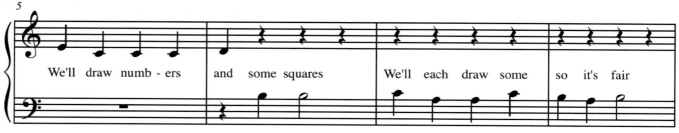

Go in - side and | get the chalk | Meet me out on | your side - walk

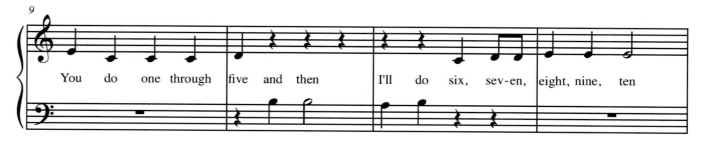

We'll draw numb - ers | and some squares | We'll each draw some | so it's fair

You do one through | five and then | I'll do six, sev-en, | eight, nine, ten

I will choose my | luck - y rock | Your turn next Let's | go Hop Scotch!

Artwork © 2016 Suzan Stroud

Music © 2010 Suzan Stroud

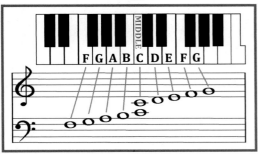

SIMON SAYS

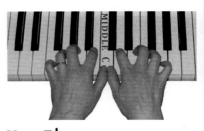

New Note F ↓

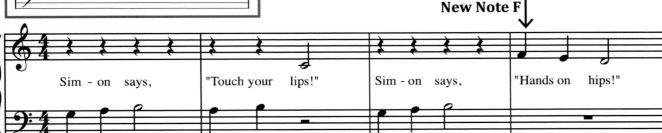

Sim - on says, | "Touch your lips!" | Sim - on says, | "Hands on hips!"

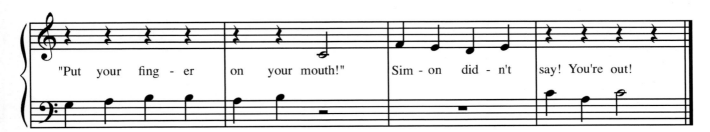

"Put your fing - er | on your mouth!" | Sim - on did - n't | say! You're out!

- **Add F in treble clef to your flash cards.**

"Simon Says" on the Keys.

1. **Teacher plays a melody on the piano.**   2. **Student plays it back using the same fingers.**

Right Hand

Left Hand

Teacher/Parent Pointers:
  - *Design melodies to help student see patterns, work on dexterity and build good finger numbers.*

     33

TIC TAC TOE

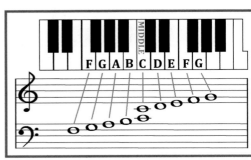

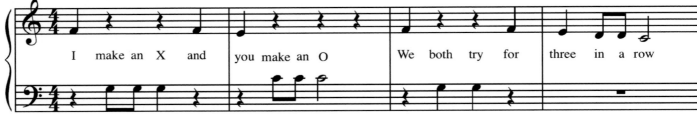

I make an X and | you make an O | We both try for | three in a row

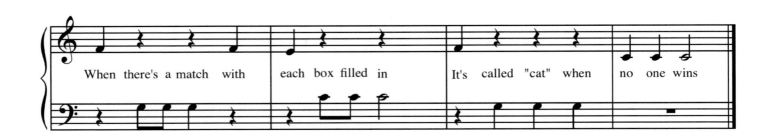

When there's a match with | each box filled in | It's called "cat" when | no one wins

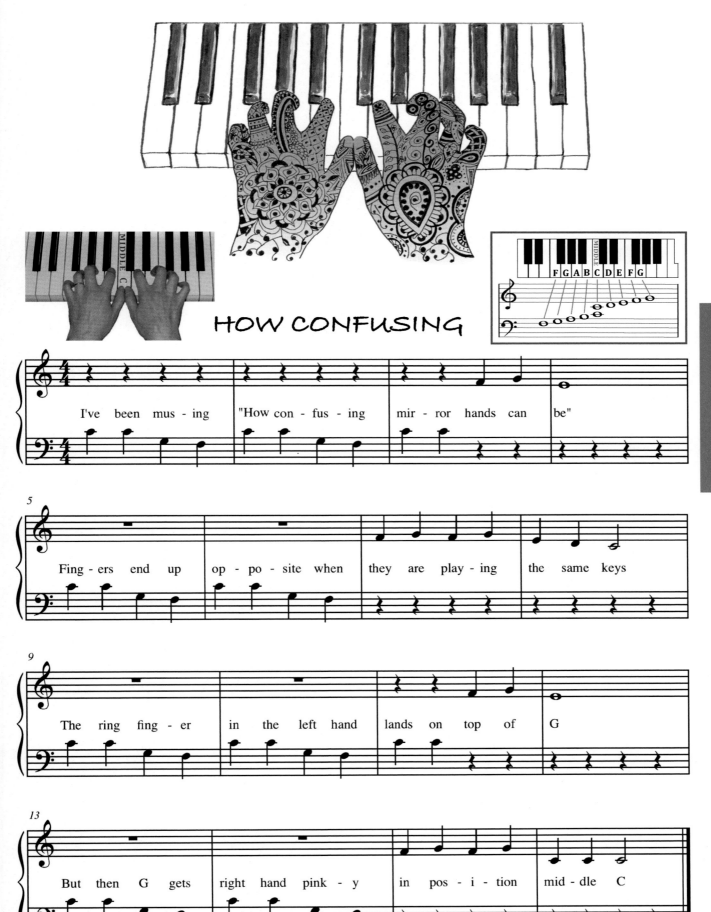

HOW CONFUSING

I've been mus - ing "How con - fus - ing mir - ror hands can be"

Fing - ers end up op - po - site when they are play - ing the same keys

The ring fing - er in the left hand lands on top of G

But then G gets right hand pink - y in pos - i - tion mid - dle C

YANKEE DOODLE

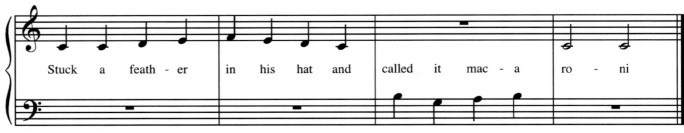

Yan - kee Dood - le went to town rid - ding on a pon - y

Stuck a feath - er in his hat and called it mac - a ro - ni

LONDON BRIDGE

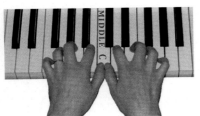

𝅘𝅥. **DOTTED QUARTER NOTE = 1 ¹/₂ counts**

Lon - don bridge is fall - ing down Fall - ing down fall - ing down
1 & 2 & 3 & 4 & 1 2 3 4 1 2 3 4 1 2 3 4

Lon - don bridge is fall - ing down My fair la - dy
1 & 2 & 3 & 4 & 1 2 3 4 1 2 3 4 1 2 3 4

- Put boxes around counts to show what counts go with each note.
  Example: 𝅘𝅥. 𝅘𝅥𝅮𝅘𝅥 𝅘𝅥
  1 & 2 & 3 & 4 &

37

TWINKLE, TWINKLE

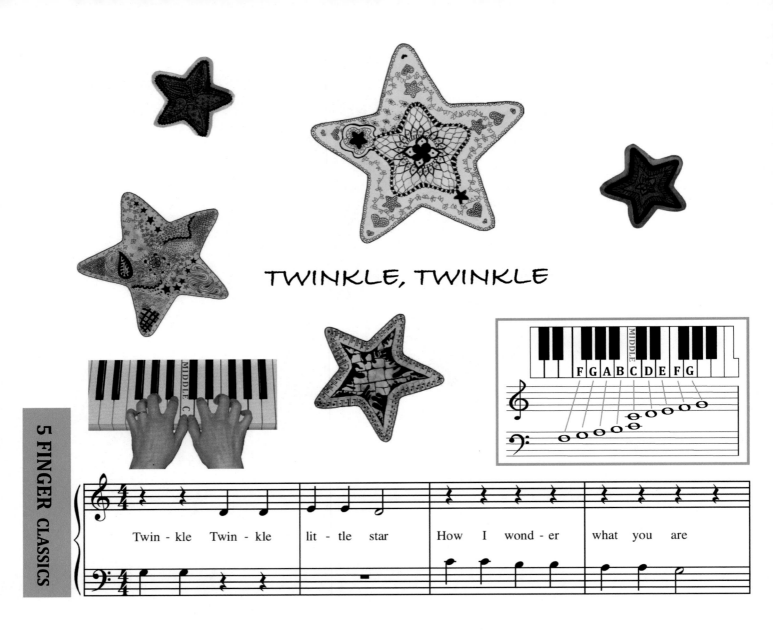

Twin - kle Twin - kle | lit - tle star | How I wond - er | what you are

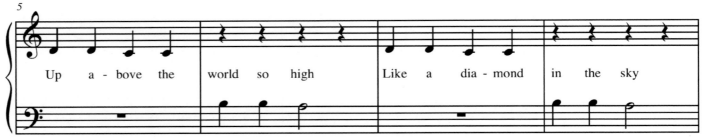

5

Up a - bove the | world so high | Like a dia - mond | in the sky

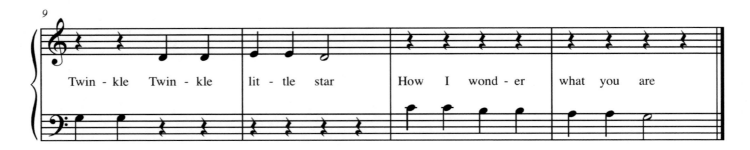

9

Twin - kle Twin - kle | lit - tle star | How I wond - er | what you are

38

HUSH LITTLE BABY

5 FINGER CLASSICS

F G A B C D E F G

Hush lit-tle ba - by | Don't say a word | Dad-dy's gon-na buy you a | mock-ing bird

If that mock - ing | bird won't sing | Dad-dy's gon-na buy you a | dia-mond ring

39

I'M A LITTLE TEAPOT

I'm a lit-tle tea-pot short and stout Here is my hand-le here is my spout

♩. **DOTTED QUARTER NOTE = 1 ¹/₂ counts** ↓

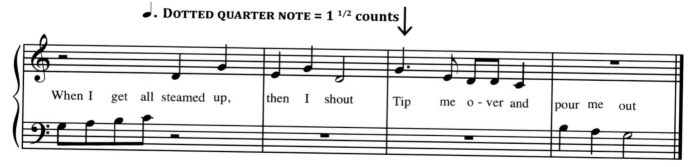

When I get all steamed up, then I shout Tip me o-ver and pour me out

40

Artwork © 2016 Suzan Stroud

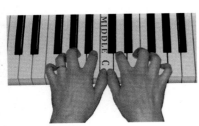

MUFFIN MAN

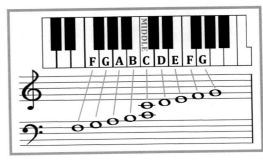

Do you know the muff-in man, the muff-in man, the muff-in man

Do you know the muff-in man that lives on Drur-y lane

♩. **DOTTED QUARTER NOTE = 1 ¹/₂ counts**

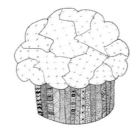

SHOO FLY

Shoo fly, don't both – er me, Shoo fly, don't both – er me

Shoo fly, don't both – er me, For I be – long to some – bod – y I

feel, I feel, I feel, I feel like morn – ing star I

feel, I feel, I feel I feel like morn – ing star

♩. **DOTTED QUARTER NOTE = 1 ¹/₂ counts**

Artwork © 2016 Suzan Stroud

TEN LITTLE INDIANS

One lit-tle, two lit-tle, three lit-tle, In-dians Four lit-tle, five lit-tle, six lit-tle, In-dians

Se-ven lit-tle, eight lit-tle, nine lit-tle, In-dians Ten In-dian Boys and Girls

HANDS TOGETHER IN C POSITION

Right Hand Thumb on Middle C

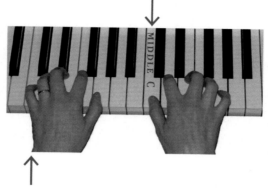

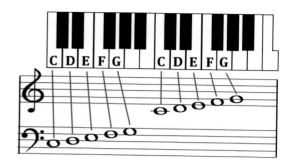

Left Hand Pinky on C below Middle C

• When the notes line up, they are played together.

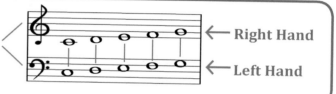

← Right Hand

← Left Hand

CHORD OUTLINE

LEFT HAND CHORDS FOR NEXT SONGS

• **This is a simplified C chord**
  (root position, no 3rd)

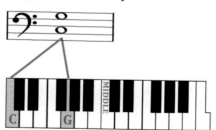

• **This is a simplified G7 chord**
  (1st inversion no 3rd, no 5th)

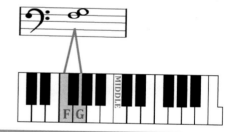

CHORD

THREE OR MORE NOTES PLAYED AT THE SAME TIME THAT CREATE A HARMONY.

• **Chords come from their scale. Example: C major chord = 1st, 3rd and 5th notes of C major scale.**
• **There are different kinds of chords with different sounds and formulas for making them.**
• **Chords can be played with notes left out (like above).**
• **Chords can be played with the notes arranged in different orders (called inversions).**

Go ahead and learn C major Scale and Chord if you haven't already!
Instructions on learning Scales and Chords are included in "Treblemakers Piano Tools".

DON'T FORGET   3 IMPORTANT HABITS TO LEARN!   DON'T FORGET

1. **KEEP FINGERS IN PROPER POSITION AS YOU PLAY:** One finger per key, right hand thumb on Middle C. Use the finger that is already on the key you need! Don't switch!
2. **CONNECT YOUR NOTES:** Don't lift between notes! Transfer weight from one finger to the next like a seesaw. Don't let the last key up until after you've pressed down the next key.
3. **DON'T WRITE NOTE NAMES IN ON YOUR SONGS:** This prevents you from getting note-reading practice.

- **Put hands in C position.**

CATS ARE

- Notes that line up get played at the same time.
- Draw a line between notes that line up.

CHORD OUTLINE

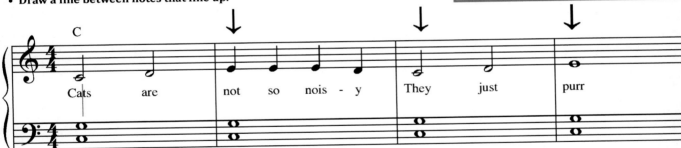

Cats are not so nois - y They just purr

Dogs are kind of bark - y and they grrrr!

- **When a letter is written over your music, it tells you what chord is being played on that beat.**

• Label the Chords. (Hint: Look at Cats Are)

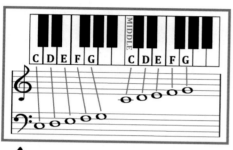

BARK! BARK!
BARK!

Bark bark bark | bow wow wow | Bark bark woof woof | bow wow wow

Bark shush bark shush | woof woof hush | Dog - gie please be | qui - et now

46   Artwork © 2016 Suzan Stroud

BUTTERFLY

CHORD OUTLINE

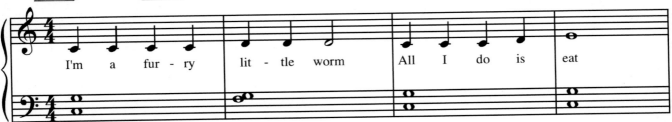

I'm a fur-ry | lit-tle worm | All I do is | eat

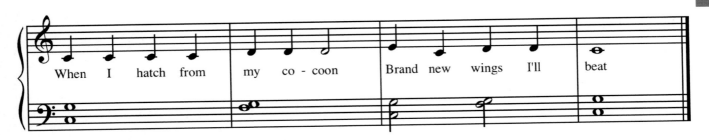

When I hatch from | my co-coon | Brand new wings I'll | beat

- Label the Chords. (Hint: Look at Cats Are)

MARY HAD A LITTLE LAMB

CHORD OUTLINE

Mar - y had a | lit - tle lamb | lit - tle lamb | lit - tle lamb

Mar - y had a | lit - tle lamb its | fleece as white as | snow

TIE: A line place between two notes that are the same pitch telling the player to hit the note once and hold it for the combined value of both notes rather than playing the note twice.

48

WAR DRUMS

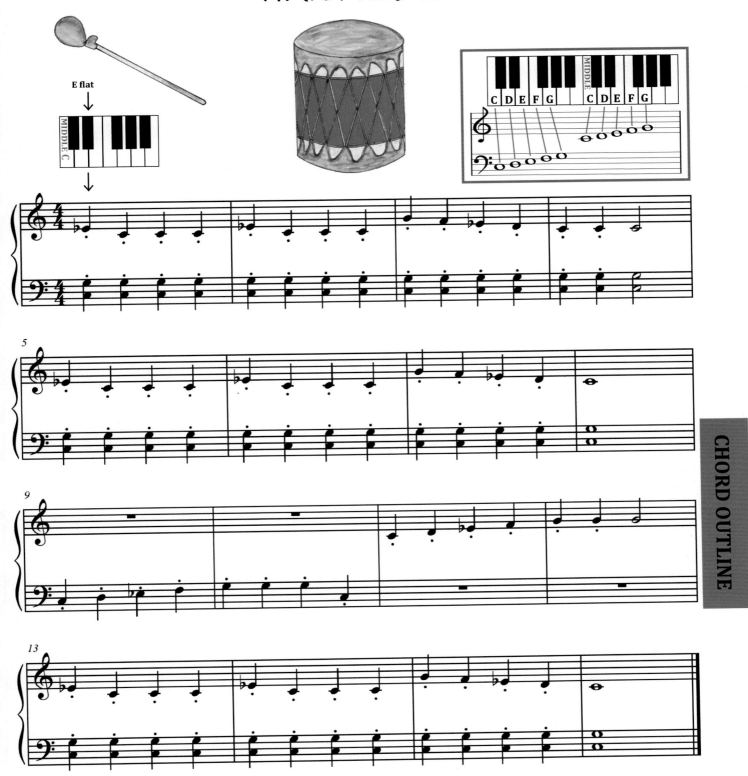

FLAT: ♭ Placed in front of a note to lower it by a half step. Affects only this specific pitch (not higher or lower notes of same letter). Lasts for rest of measure.

STACCATO: ♩ A dot that is placed over or under the notehead to show that the note should be played short and disconnected from the note after it.

Music © 2010 Suzan Stroud

DYNAMICS:

Louds and softs used in music to create contrast and express emotion.

SYMBOL	STANDS FOR	MEANS	EXAMPLE
ppp	Pianississimo	Very, very soft	Whispering
pp	Pianissimo	Very soft	Almost at a whisper
p	Piano	Soft	Softer than speaking voice
mp	Mezzo Piano	Moderately soft	Speaking voice
mf	Mezzo Forte	Moderately loud	
f	Forte	Loud	Louder than speaking
ff	Fortissimo	Very loud	Speaking loud
fff	Fortississimo	Very, very loud	Yelling
sf	Sforzando	Loud and accented	Drill Sergeant
<	Crescendo	Gradually get louder	
>	Decrescendo or Diminuendo	Gradually get softer	
>	Accent	A stress or emphasis given to a note	

ODE TO JOY

♩. **Dotted quarter note = 1 ½ counts**

CHORD OUTLINE

rit. **RITARDANDO: Gradually slow down.**

Artwork © 2016 Suzan Stroud 51

- Recognizing patterns and Chord shapes makes Reading music easier.
- Songs in this section move up and down together in PARALELL MOTION.

WATCH ME READ

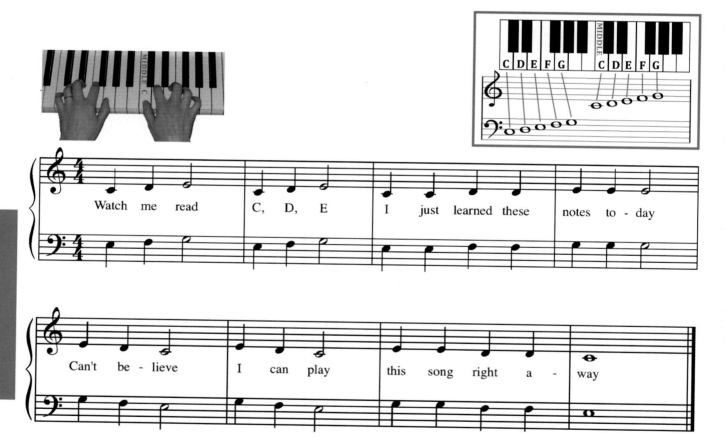

Watch me read | C, D, E | I just learned these | notes to - day

Can't be - lieve | I can play | this song right a - way

PARALLEL MOTION: Both hands move in the same direction using the same intervals.
INTERVALS: Distance between two notes.

BUBBLES

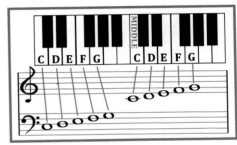

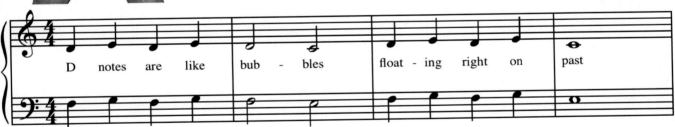

D notes are like bub – bles float – ing right on past

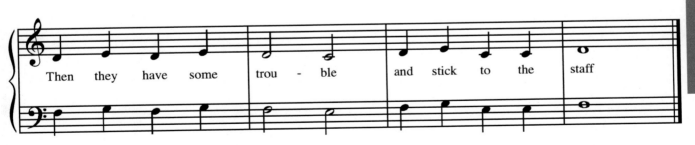

Then they have some trou – ble and stick to the staff

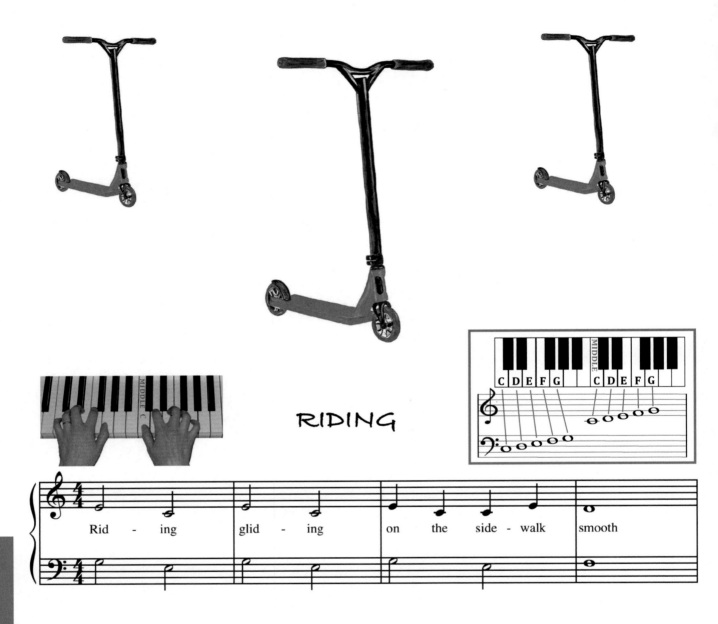

RIDING

Rid - ing glid - ing on the side - walk smooth

I am fly - ing scoot - er on the move

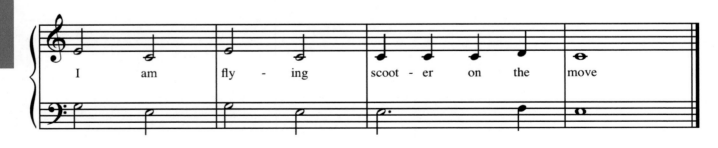

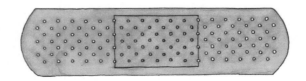

Artwork © 2016 Suzan Stroud   Music © 2010 Suzan Stroud

WEAR YOUR HELMET

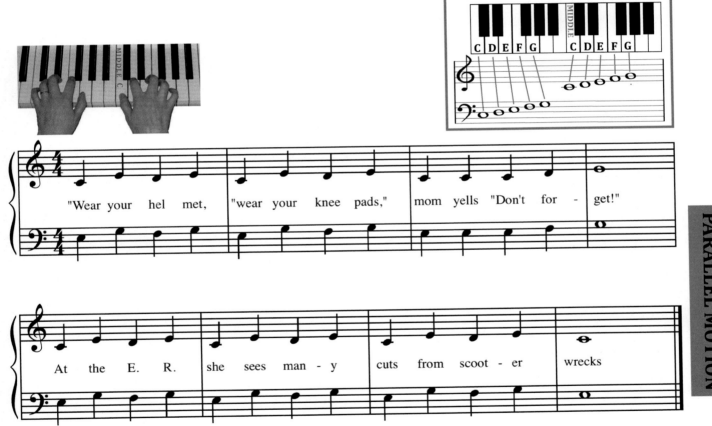

"Wear your hel met, "wear your knee pads," mom yells "Don't for - get!"

At the E. R. she sees man - y cuts from scoot - er wrecks

55

RECOGNIZING CHORD PATTERNS

CHORDS CAN BE PLAYED MANY WAYS. HERE ARE SOME EXAMPLES USING C CHORD:

With the notes all at once straight from the scale (root position):

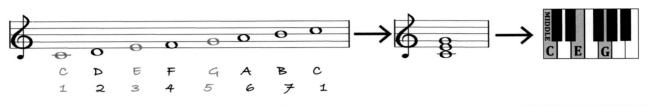

In different inversions:
(notes of chord in a different order)

Outline of chord with notes left out:

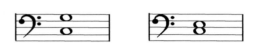

Notes of chord played separately:

Chords Split up:

CHORD PATTERN

In this section we will begin to recognize some of these patterns.
>   To make it easier we will:
>   • Only work with the two chords we introduced earlier: C and G7.
>   • Only have chord patterns in your left hand.

The chord patterns may: use some of the notes, have rearranged notes, or both.
They could be played at the same time or separately.

C chord	C chord (outline)	G7 chord	Simplified G7 chord
(C,E,G)	(C,G)	(G,B,D,F)	(F,G)

STEP RIGHT UP

Step right up   Step right down   Hop and skip a   key

Look   for   step-ping   Look   for   skip-ping   It   can   help   you   read

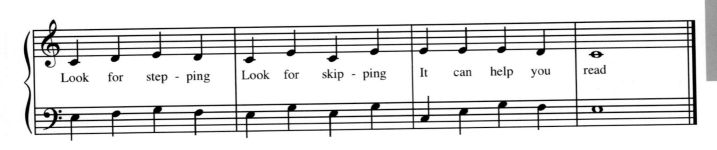

CHORD PATTERN

STEPPING, SKIPPING OR THE SAME

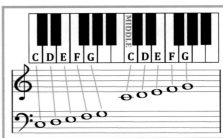

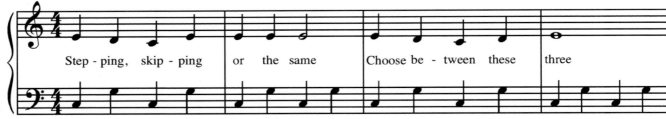

> Step - ping, skip - ping | or the same | Choose be - tween these | three
>
> Can you tell the | dif - ference be - tween | all the notes you | see

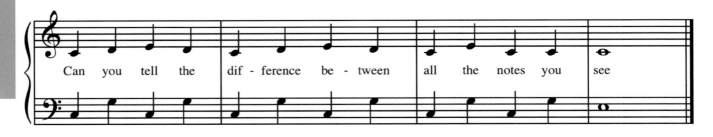

ROW YOUR BOAT

TIME SIGNATURE: Top Number = 6 beats per measure
Bottom Number = ♪ Eighth Note gets the beat

Row, row, row your boat Gent - ly down the stream
1 2 3 4 5 6 1 2 3 4 5 6 1 2 3 4 5 6 1 2 3 4 5 6

New Note C

Mer - ri - ly mer - ri - ly mer - ri - ly mer - ri - ly Life is but a dream
1 2 3 4 5 6 1 2 3 4 5 6 1 2 3 4 5 6 1 2 3 4 5 6

CHORD PATTERN

TIME SIGNATURE: Top number tells how many counts in each measure.
Bottom number tells what note gets the beat.

4 = quarter note ♩ • 2 = half note ♩ • 8 = eighth note ♪ • 16 = sixteenth note ♬

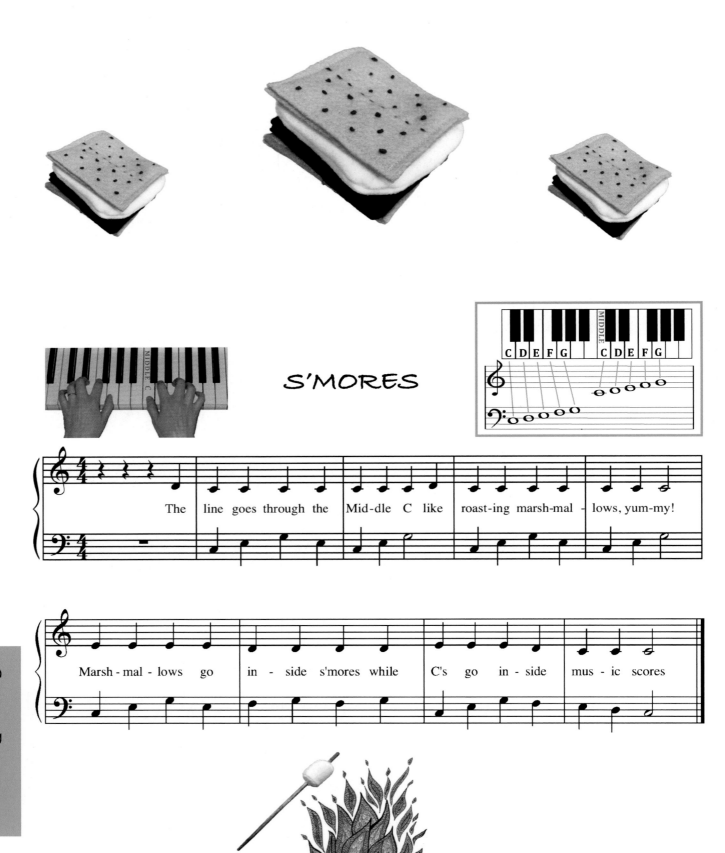

S'MORES

The line goes through the Mid-dle C like roast-ing marsh-mal - lows, yum-my!

Marsh - mal - lows go in - side s'mores while C's go in - side mus - ic scores

TWO SMALL SNAILS

↓ **3 counts per measure**

Two small snails Dance the min - u - et

New Note B ↑

Slug - gy heads held high They cause all snails to sigh

Shells move in time Grace - ful as they slime

Most ma - jes - ti - cally They do their steps in

three

Music © 2010 Suzan Stroud

CHORD PATTERN

61

RHYTHM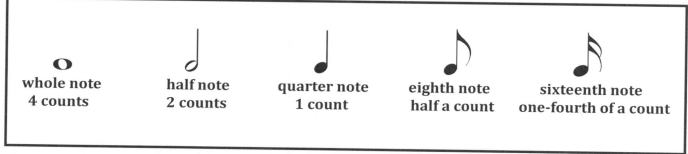

- Remember, each line and space on the staff stands for a note on the piano.
- What *kind* of note is used tells how long to hold it.

O whole note 4 counts	𝅗𝅥 half note 2 counts	♩ quarter note 1 count	♪ eighth note half a count	♬ sixteenth note one-fourth of a count

- Go ahead and add o 𝅗𝅥 ♩ to your flash cards. (don't add ♪ yet)

Lets try some rhythms!

- Rhythm is like a picture of time going by from left to right.
- Put a box around the counts that go with each note. (example below)

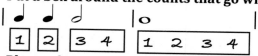

- Play and count in time (Student may need to point to the notes and count first).

This is a time signature:
- Top number tells how many counts per measure.
- Bottom number tells what note gets the beat.

4 = quarter note ♩ (1/4) • 2 = half note 𝅗𝅥 (1/2) • 8 = eighth note ♪ (1/8) • 16 = sixteenth note ♪ (1/16)

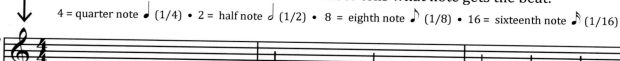

- When more than one eighth or sixteenth note (or any flagged notes) happen in a row, they get beamed into groups.
- This makes it easier to see beat groupings.

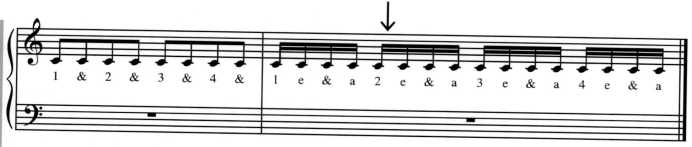

- **Add to your songs.** (Write counts in each measure, box the numbers, then play and count out loud.)

- **When you can play the rhythms smoothly, add the metronome.**

For more in-depth explanation of **Rhythm** and **Time Signature** see "Treblemakers Piano Tools" Music

RHYTHM